Islands of Wonder
MAUI

Text by **Tom Stevens**

Photography by **Douglas Peebles**

Mutual Publishing

Library of Congress Control Number: 2011936095
ISBN-10: 1-56647-961-4
ISBN-13: 978-1-56647-961-5

First Printing, July 2012
Second Printing, September 2015
Designed by Courtney Young

Mutual Publishing, LLC
1215 Center Street, Suite 210
Honolulu, Hawai'i 96816
Ph: 808-732-1709 / Fax: 808-734-4094
email: info@mutualpublishing.com
www.mutualpublishing.com
Printed in China

INTRODUCTION

Maui is many islands in one. In a single day, you can travel to rain forests, mountains, valleys and deserts. An island of flowers can be found here, another of trees, another of waterfalls. The beaches alone could be several islands, one for each color of sand: red, white, black, green, and gold.

Douglas Peebles has photographed these various Mauis for many years, and this book collects some of his finest work. Whether shooting from air, sea or shore, he views each scene from an explorer's perspective, as if seeing it for the first time.

This gives his images startling vividness and clarity. Viewing them here, readers who know Maui well, as well as those meeting the island for the first time will be equally delighted and surprised.

A sense of wonder is also evident as Peebles discovers and honors the island. Whether his image is a whimsical roadside stand, a canoe team on the water, or an Edenic landscape, the photographer seems delighted and amazed to have witnessed it. That's a rare quality.

Equally rare is Peebles' ability to bring his viewers along, as if we were seeing the island through his viewfinder, or over his shoulder. This sense of shared discovery gives the photos an "up close and personal" presence as warm as a Maui welcome.

With that in mind, this book lets you explore Maui as if Douglas Peebles were your guide. Together you'll travel through several "Mauis" and view them from various perspectives. Sometimes you'll be in a helicopter; other times on a hilltop, and occasionally, in a hammock.

You'll visit Central Maui, the island's colorful commercial and recreational hub. An Upcountry loop showcases a "mountain Maui" of scenic farms and ranches. You'll drive (and fly) along the rugged Hāna Coast, where emerald rain forests meet a sapphire sea. Circuits of West Maui and South Maui explore the island's sun-kissed, surf-swept beach resorts, as magnificent as any in the world.

Many Mauis, one guide. We hope you'll enjoy the ride.

Left: Coconut palms silhouette an azure sky on a moonlit night at Wailea.
Previous page: With Moloka'i as a backdrop, two visitors head out for a morning snorkel in Kā'anapali's warm, clear waters.

CENTRAL MAUI

The island's geographic center is often overlooked by first-time visitors hastening to sunny leeward resorts. This is their loss.

Savvier travelers long ago discovered the surf-swept, cane-fringed beauty of Central Maui's aquamarine North Shore. The soulful charm of tree-shaded Wailuku and the precipitous majesty of mile-deep 'Iao Valley—the "Yosemite of the Pacific"—are equally revered. And the once sleepy plantation town of Pā'ia has become a hip arts and fashion Mecca for the international set.

As the island's cultural, commercial and government hub, populous Central Maui is as close to "city" as Maui gets. Yet mere minutes away are freshwater streams and waterfalls, subalpine meadows, live coral reefs, and cliff-side overlooks as scary as any in the Pacific.

The island's center also remains a center for extreme sports innovation. Windswept Central Maui beaches pioneered high-performance wave sailing, tow-in surfing and kite surfing.

Three windsurfers sketch the day's first wakes across the inviting waters of Central Maui's Kanahā Beach Park. On a windy day, the park hosts boardsailors and kite surfers from all over the world.

5

This page: Using their superior speed and maneuverability, windsurfers pioneered the big wave spot called Pe'ahi or Jaws. They now share the world-renowned break with "tow-in" surfers pulled by jet skis.

Opposite page, top photo: Built as a "movie palace" in 1927 and since restored, Wailuku's busy Iao Theater regularly presents plays, movies and live music. **Bottom photo:** Wearing kukui nut garlands and monarchy-era clothing styles, a Wailuku hula hālau dances with grace, poise and precision.

Following page: Rising above the stream that carved it, 'Īao Needle is the centerpiece of a steep, spectacular valley some call "the Yosemite of the Pacific."

Top photo: Named for a famous Maui queen, graceful Kaʻahumanu Church occupies a shady corner of Wailuku, the county capital. **Bottom photo:** The "swinging bridge" across Waiheʻe Stream leads hikers through a steamy rain forest to icy swimming holes.

Opposite page: Near-perfect surf and sea conditions greet two competitors in a windsurf contest at Hoʻokipa Beach Park.

Above: Shaded by ironwood trees, a spectator watches kite surfers ply the windy waters off Kanahā Beach Park. **Left:** Afternoon glare silhouettes two outrigger canoe teams and a flock of windsurf sails off Kanahā Beach Park.

Opposite page: Warm waters and strong and steady trade winds have made Central Maui's Kite Beach a Mecca for the world's top kite surfers.

WEST MAUI

From certain vantage points, West Maui actually looks like a separate island, and in many respects it is. It has its own volcano, its own river valleys, its own harbor and airport, its own world-class resorts, and its own distinctive history.

Long favored by Hawaiian royalty for its sheltered surfing beaches, sweet streams and abundant marine life, the West Maui town of Lahaina became the Hawaiian kingdom's second capitol. Those features also made Lahaina a magnet for rowdy Pacific whalers as well as the Christian missionaries who tried to tame them.

In more recent times, the development at Kāʻanapali Beach, Hawaiʻi's first master planned destination resort sparked a real estate and construction boom still going strong 50 years later. The elite Kapalua resort and numerous shoreline condominiums also have capitalized on West Maui's golden beaches, turquoise waters and dramatic mountain backdrops.

Should all that pale, historic Front Street beckons with shopping, art galleries, nightlife, restaurants and fiery lūʻau shows. The whalers may be history, but their street's still jumping.

Snorkelers surround the sailing catamaran that has ferried them to Honolua Bay, a marine reserve in summer and world-class surf break in winter.

Above: Their sunset workout finished, West Maui paddlers carry their 400-pound outrigger canoe up Hanaka'ō'ō Beach. **Left:** A roadside stand offers sweet, juicy, golden West Maui pineapples at bargain prices.

Opposite page, top photo: The photographer's wraparound lens captures a classic Honolua panorama—the palm grove, aquamarine waves, and distant Moloka'i beneath its cape of clouds. **Bottom photo:** A speeding surfer plots his next maneuver on a peeling turquoise curl at Honolua Bay.

Above, top photo: Commercial charter boats await customers at Lahaina's picturesque small boat harbor, a favorite subject for plein air painters. **Above:** An ancient mariner welcomes shipmates ashore at historic Pioneer Inn, Lahaina's venerable harbor-front hotel and tavern. **Left:** As twilight fades to black, bright storefronts, restaurants, galleries and clubs beckon passersby along Lahaina's Front Street.

Opposite page: A tour helicopter hovers like a dragonfly over the gem-like pool of this remote West Maui waterfall.

Opposite page: The cloud-capped West Maui volcano Puʻukukui overlooks waterfront homes along Lahaina's Front Street. The thirty-foot red and white "L" tattooing its side stands for Lahainaluna High School and has been maintained by the students since 1904. Lying in the lee of two volcanoes, Lahaina generally enjoys calm and sunny weather.

Left: Late afternoon sun bathes a plumeria-garlanded hula dancer at the Kāʻanapali resort.

Below: Bathed in floodlights, the Kāʻanapali resort readies for twilight dining, dancing and dinner shows.

Right: A graceful hula dancer fronts an island trio for a sunset performance on a Kāʻanapali hotel terrace.

Below: Once known as "Slaughterhouse," for a nearby ranch building, Mokulēʻia Beach is a favorite destination for body surfers and boogie boarders.

Opposite page: The seaside hotels and condominiums of the Kāʻanapali resort cast morning shadows across a pair of early beachcombers.

Left: Rain squalls out at sea promise showers for the residents of scenic Kahakuloa Village.

Below: If ʻĪao Valley is Maui's Yosemite, Kahakuloa is its Gibraltar. The rock's steep bluffs guard a stream and Hawaiian farming village accessible by a narrow, slippery, serpentine road.

Opposite page: Lovingly restored, repainted and reroofed by parishioners, this old village church at Kahakuloa is a longtime West Maui landmark.

Above: A bather gazes from Kā'anapali Beach as the sun sets behind Lāna'i. In times past, the placid "roadstead" offshore has harbored whaling ships and the U.S. Pacific Fleet.

Right: Eons of erosive wave action create "blow holes" in the lava, like this one at Nākālele. Caverns beneath the rock convert incoming waves into geyser-like blasts of spray.

Opposite page: Coconut palms seem to reach toward the setting sun at Launiupoko Beach Park, a popular surf spot and picnic destination. Lāna'i island lies ten miles distant.

SOUTH MAUI

By reputation, South Maui is the newest of the Mauis, but like the youngest child, this one has many admirers. It wasn't always so. While its long beaches landed war parties and fishing canoes in ancient times, the region's scarcity of potable water seemed likely to limit future prospects.

That changed in 1975, when four major landowners bankrolled a pipeline that sent West Maui well water coursing across the arid badlands of Kīhei, Wailea and Mākena. Overnight, the South Maui desert blossomed into a "gold coast" of world class resorts, golf courses, retail malls and celebrity spas.

Unchanged were the region's scenic assets. Mākena's pristine Oneloa Beach remains a Mecca for sunbathers and wave riders. A few miles offshore, tiny Molokini islet offers 200-foot visibility and amazing marine life. Basking like whales on the glittering horizon are Kahoʻolawe, Lānaʻi and Molokaʻi.

And every evening, the Gold Coast presents at no charge whatsoever Hawaiʻi's longest and fieriest sunsets. Enjoy!

An aerial view shows the Wailea resort in the foreground, the Maui Meadows community in the middle distance, and the cloud-wreathed

This page: Backed by condominiums but open to the public, Wailea's placid Mōkapu Beach is a favorite among families with young children.

Opposite page, top photo: Young coconut palms offer cool, shadowy relief from the afternoon ocean glare. Molokini islet can be seen in the foreground of larger, fainter Kaho'olawe. **Bottom photo:** Day's end bathes Wailea Beach in a palette of pastels. South Maui sunsets and seascapes are popular subjects for isle painters.

Right: Upraised flukes and a "blow" of breath announce a pair of humpback whales off the South Maui coast.

Below: The clear, shallow waters off South Maui host up to 3,000 migrating humpback whales each winter and spring. The whales mate and calve in Hawai'i, then return to Alaska to feed.

Opposite page: A palm-tree hammock at Wailea Beach offers this couple a carefree view of a dinner cruise boat silhouetted by the sunset.

Following pages: Also called "Big Beach" and "Oneloa" (long sand), pristine Mākena Beach is South Maui's most popular destination.

Opposite page: The golden sands and sapphire seas of Kīhei's Kama'ole Beach Parks await bathers on a crystal-clear morning. From this vantage, distant West Maui seems like another island.

Above: Six-person outrigger canoes await paddlers at the Kīhei Canoe Club site on Sugar Beach. The gently curving three-mile shoreline between Kīhei and Mā'alaea is also popular with beachcombers and joggers.

Right: The quaint Keolahau Congregational Church recalls Kīhei's earlier history as a Hawaiian fishing and trading community.

This page: The fine-grained sand at Wailea's Ulua Beach is ideal for impromptu sand sculptures. The beach also hosts yearly contests for serious artisans.

Opposite page, top photo: Sailboats anchor in shallow seas off South Maui's Kīhei coast, a vantage for some of the island's longest, most smoldering sunsets. **Bottom photo:** The footprints of early morning walkers stipple palm-shadowed Keawakapu Beach. Cloud-capped West Maui is visible in the distance.

Brilliant South Maui sunsets can trick the eye. Here Molokini islet, center,
seems a headland of much larger Kaho'olawe. In reality, they are miles apart.

This page: The sequestered inlets and fresh water ponds of the 'Āhihi-Cape Kīna'u Natural Area Reserve await hikers who trek across rugged lava terrain south of Mākena.

Opposite page: Once a cinder cone on the slopes of an older, larger Maui, Molokini islet is now half-submerged. The rock crescent shelters an extraordinary marine ecosystem where reef and pelagic species mingle in crystal clear water.

UPCOUNTRY

As one of the "high islands" in the Pacific, 10,000-foot Maui confounds many expectations. We're in the tropics, true, but it can snow here. Out one window you may see cactus, out another, redwood trees.

If those traversing the alpine meadows and dry forests of Maui's "Upcountry" region could ignore the surrounding ocean (good luck), they might think they were in Montana. Cowboys ride mile-high fence lines past grazing cattle. Pheasants and quail startle from the underbrush. Jacarandas shed purple flowers in a cool mountain breeze.

This Maui houses the Pacific's most dramatic caldera: vast, moonlike, cone-studded Haleakalā. Here also are flower and produce farms, horse paddocks, cloud forests and breathtaking views. For first-time visitors expecting the South Seas, Upcountry Maui is an indelible surprise.

This region also nurtures innovation. It is a nexus for creative artists, scientists, performers and thinkers. Its astronomers probe the heavens, its geologists take the planet's pulse. Its farmers develop new flowers, new coffees, sweeter onions.

Now that's sweet.

When you've got this much acreage to mow, it's best to sit down. This Makawao estate borders Maui's vast Haleakalā Ranch. The purple tree is a jacaranda, an Upcountry favorite.

Above: Named for the French explorer who witnessed one of Haleakalā's final eruptions, La Pérouse Bay shelters in the dark arms of Cape Kīna'u, a lava peninsula that spilled out into the sea.

Right: A smaller variant of the Canada Goose, Hawai'i's handsome but endangered nēnē can most often be seen on the slopes of Haleakalā.

Opposite page: The rare silversword plants at Haleakalā's summit bloom only once, raising a column of sticky red blossoms for optimal seed dispersal. Once used in lei-making, the silversword is now a protected species.

Left: The visitor center at Haleakalā's summit is a popular scenic stop.

Below: On a sunny day, the vastness of Haleakalā seems to lazily float in a bubble bath of clouds. Swirling cinder patterns mark the routes of ancient lava flows. Colorful, eroding cliffs lend an Old West aspect befitting the mountain's ranching heritage.

Opposite page: The road to Haleakalā's 10,000-foot summit forms a series of serpentine curves as it zigzags up the mountain. On clear days, motorists can see four other islands from this road.

Right: A graceful stand of jacaranda trees adds rich royal purple highlights along the upper Kula highway. Spring is the best time to enjoy these colorful, fragrant trees.

Below: 'Ulupalakua Ranch cloaks the cone-studded southwest shoulder of Haleakalā in an emerald mantle of pasture grass and eucalyptus forest.

Opposite page: A curious horse peers over the fence of a green and shady Kēōkea pasture.

This page: Rising far above sea level, Upcountry Maui hosts a broad array of native and introduced flora. Among the latter is this dramatic passion flower vine.

Opposite page, top left photo Powdery volcanic soils, crisp weather and abundant sunshine make the Upcountry district of Kula a natural site for flower farms. **Top right photo:** A "pin cushion" protea blossom. **Bottom photo:** This Kula bouquet includes several varieties of protea, exotic plants named for a shape-shifting Greek sea god. Introduced to Kula on an experimental basis in the 1960s, protea farming is now a thriving local enterprise.

Hanging in clusters from dense vines, blue jade flowers are highly prized for lei making.

Majestic cypresses and pines form a scenic windbreak for this vegetable farm. Kula's powdery soil, warm days and cool nights are ideal for many crops.

HĀNA COAST

Long before Maui became a household word, its sublime Hāna Coast was a haven for celebrities, heiresses and captains of industry. Movie stars vacationed here unrecognized and undisturbed. Corporate CEO's built retirement homes here. And the most famous American of his generation—Charles Lindbergh—lived, died and was buried here.

The simple reason for all this is that the Hāna Coast is unique, and that uniqueness has been recognized for centuries. This was the birthplace of Hawaiian royalty, the prize of ancient battles, and home to the highest of high priests.

Those times have passed, but the verdant Hāna Coast remains Hawai'i's "most Hawaiian place." From the lush banana groves and taro patches of misty Ke'anae to the lofty jungle waterfalls of Kīpahulu and Kaupō, this is as Polynesian as Hawai'i gets.

Islanders call Hāna the pōhaku, the foundation stone of their being. For beneath the lava cliffs and rain-fed pools, the hidden beaches and bamboo groves beats the living heart of an ancient culture.

With a sparkling blue bay before it and emerald green hills behind, Hāmoa is among Maui's most scenic beaches.

Above: Crowned by coconut trees, craggy 'Ālau Island guards the Hāna coast at Hāmoa, site of an old Hawaiian fish pond. A common inquiry: how did those coconut trees get up there?

Right: Rainfall coursing down Haleakalā waters the taro ponds and banana groves of misty Wailua Valley.

Opposite page: Ti plants, breadfruit trees and kukui trees frame Wailua Falls near the Ke'anae Peninsula.

This page: Like a window to an older Hawai'i, Ke'anae peninsula offers views of taro ponds, banana groves and stately coconut palms. Waves crashing along the cliffs send a fine salt mist into the air.

Opposite page, top photo: As if by prior agreement, rain, wind and sun meet daily along the Hāna Coast to create some of Hawai'i's loveliest rainbows. **Bottom photo:** A papaya tree heavy with ripening fruit stands before the stream that waters it.

Above, left photo: Garlanded in plumeria, a hula dancer kneels beside her instruments. The ipu hand drum above is a dried and tempered squash gourd. The 'uli'ulī rattle at right is slit bamboo. **Right photo:** Hula practitioners greet the sunrise with a Hawaiian chant at historic Pi'ilanihale, an ancient royal temple site.

Right: Hāna residents use a lay net and an inner tube to harvest a silvery catch for the town's annual Taro Festival.

Opposite page: Carved into sheer cliffs, the Hāna road snakes through the dense East Maui rainforest hundreds of feet above the Pacific.

This page: At the aptly named Garden of Eden Botanic Gardens and Arboretum, bright ti and heliconia plants ring a stone pool for water lilies and papyrus reeds

Opposite page, top photo: Before the road to Hāna was built, horses and canoes provided access to this rugged coast. The road is just visible slanting along the cliffs behind this Ke'anae steed.
Bottom photo: Long a Kīpahulu landmark, the whimsical "baby pigs crossing" sign has starred in a million shapshots and even a few works of art

64

Thrill seekers leap from this bridge into one of the famous "Seven Sacred Pools" in the 'Ohe'o Gulch at Kīpahulu, where Haleakalā National Park meets the sea.

Left: Shaggy hala trees frame a surf-churned Hāna Coast seascape. Stripped of their thorny edges, the tough, pliable hala leaves are woven into mats, hats and even canoe sails. **Below:** Volcanic black sands meet clear, sapphire blue waters in a cove at Wai'ānapanapa state park.

Opposite page, top left: Family fruit stands like this one are well worth a pullout on the drive to Hāna. Featured here are pineapples, bananas, passion fruit and starfruit, all fresh daily. **Top right:** A surfboard mileage marker shares the frame with an equally colorful anthurium bloom along the Hāna Road at Nāhiku. **Bottom photo:** A short walk up a paved trail offers a view of Hāna town, its small harbor, and its landmark Ka'uiki Hill, birthplace of royalty.

This page: Features of the rugged Hāna Coast not visible to motorists are accessible on most days by air, and on a few days by sea.

Following page: An aerial photo captures motorists in a classic Hāna Road moment: crossing a narrow bridge past a waterfall and freshwater pool.

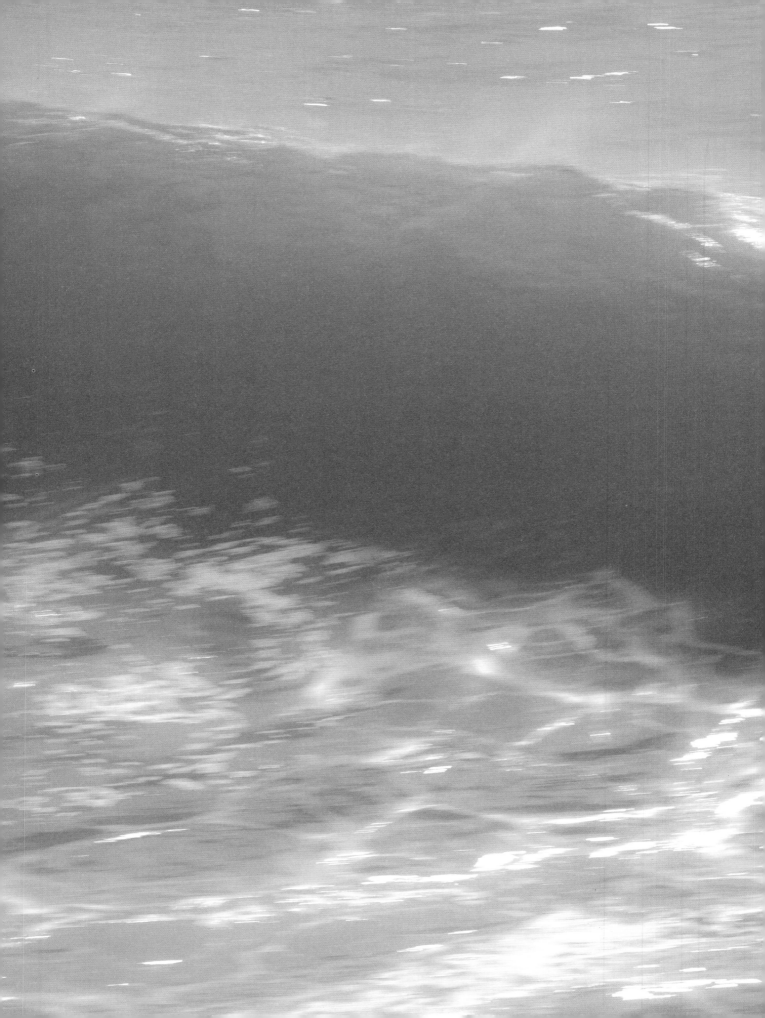